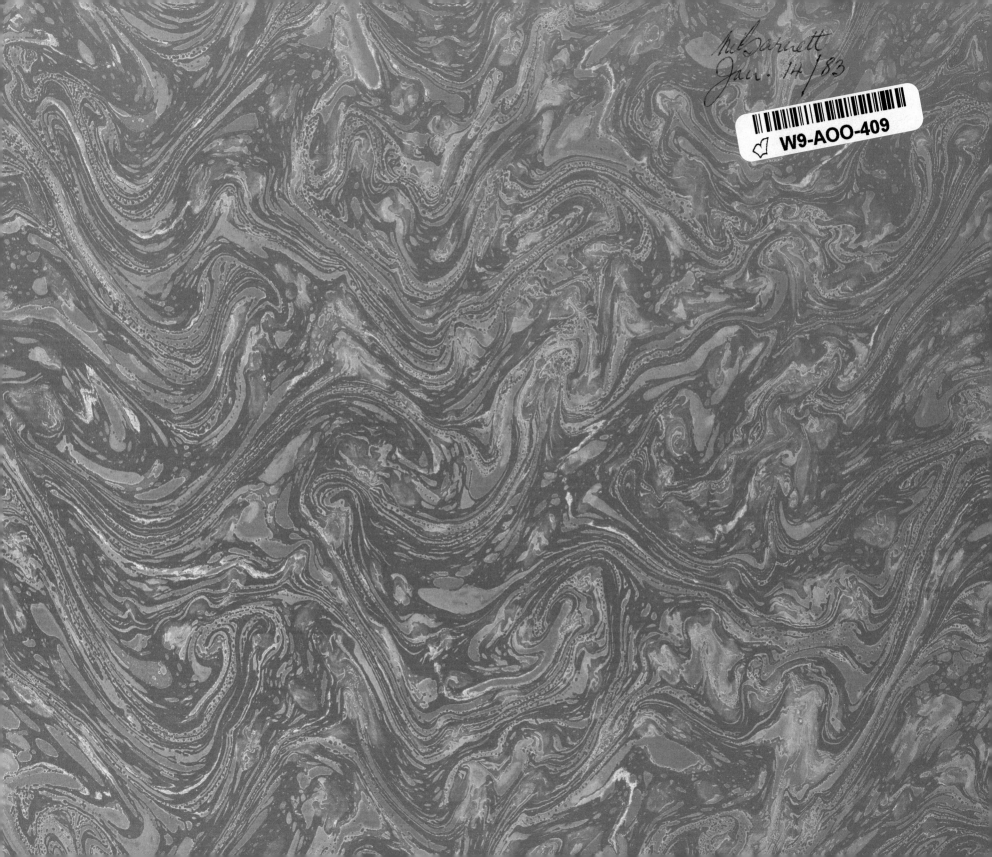

An Edwardian Observer

AN EDWARDIAN OBSERVER

The Photographs of Leslie Hamilton Wilson

Introduction by Edwin Newman   Text by Clark Worswick

Edited by Marilyn Penn

A Pennwick/Crown Book

In doing this brief account of the work of Leslie Hamilton Wilson, I received invaluable assistance and suggestions from various people. I would like to thank W. D. Grant and Allan McLeod in Scotland for such background as they could provide on the subject. Both Valerie Lloyd and Paul Katz offered objective opinions about Wilson which proved helpful in the course of assembling this book. Harold Landry provided a convenient yardstick by which to measure the posthumous value of Wilson's work. Brom Anderson proferred perceptive editorial comments on the manuscript. But without the support of Lawrence and Martha Friedricks, and the interest and enthusiasm of Arthur Penn, the work of Leslie Hamilton Wilson would never have been discovered or published. Marilyn Penn did much more than edit this book; she collaborated with me in seeking to find an accurate description of Wilson and his place in the history of photography. Any conclusions and their particular merit, are joint conclusions which could not have been reached without her contribution and uncommon care. To Joan, my wife, I owe a great debt for always believing. I should like to dedicate this book to her.

—Clark Worswick

"Cargoes" and "Roadways" by John Masefield are reprinted with permission of
Macmillan Publishing Co., Inc., copyright 1912, renewed 1940 by
John Masefield. "The Wild Swans at Coole" from *The Collected Poems of
William Butler Yeats* is reprinted with permission of Macmillan Publishing Co.,
Inc., copyright 1919, renewed 1947 by Bertha Georgie Yeats.

Library of Congress Catalogue Card No. 78-69844
ISBN: Clothbound 0-517-533766

Copyright, © Pennwick Publishing Inc., 1978
Manufactured in the United States of America

Book Design by Michael Flanagan

Contents

Introduction

When I arrived in England in 1949, George VI was on the throne. He was, by all accounts, an amiable, well-meaning man, but greatly handicapped as a public figure by a stammer. He had, of course, become King through the abdication of his brother, Edward VIII, and although thirteen years had gone by, and the Second World War had been fought, he seemed, much of the time, more the caretaker of the monarchy than its embodiment.

When Elizabeth II succeeded him in 1953, there was a wistful and self-conscious attempt by the press, trying to enlarge the story, and by others, who hoped that somehow the new reign would bring a new flowering of British vigor and inventiveness, to have it become known as the Second Elizabethan Age. The attempt failed. There were no new Elizabethans. If the period is to be called Elizabethan, it will have to be done in retrospect, by the historians. This, it is true, is the usual way, but it was more likely to happen when the period had a homogeneity, a definable and recognizable quality, and when Britain's pre-eminence was acknowledged by the rest of the world. The reign of Edward VII (1901-1910) met those requirements as firmly as did his mother's. So it was that the Victorian Age was followed by the Edwardian.

We know now that during the Edwardian Age, forces were in being in Asia, Africa, North America, Europe, that were to destroy Britain's certainty that it was the best of all countries, proud, wise and unassailable, and which rapidly and drastically reduced its influence in the world. We know that in Britain itself, dissatisfaction with things as they were was taking political form. Shaw was at work, and H. G. Wells, and the Webbs, and Fabian socialism and the Labor Party (founded in 1906) were beginning their march toward power in Westminster.

But in the Edwardian period, this was apparent only to the prophetic, who must have seemed less prophetic than cranky. To the vast majority, Britain was the world's leading power not only because of its wealth and might and sagacity, but also because that was right and proper, preordained, as it should be. It was no accident that Sir Edward Elgar composed his "Pomp and Circumstance" marches between 1902 and 1907.

The King himself—King-Emperor, to take account of the Indian Empire—personified this. He did not have the unique social eminence the Queen has today. He did receive "the deference due to me" (to borrow a phrase from a celebrated figure of the Victorian and Edwardian periods, W. S. Gilbert) but the opulence of his life was approached by that of dozens of men, and perhaps equalled and even surpassed by some. The names—Derby, Rosebery, Marlborough, Rothschild, and the rest—are still familiar. Stately homes were not turned into tourist attractions in those days to save their proprietors from bankruptcy. Edwardian high society meant grandee millionaire after grandee millionaire. The riches of the Empire poured in. Somebody, seeing London for the first time, said, "What a city to loot!"

Edward VII by no means set a high moral or intellectual tone. As Prince of Wales, he was involved in scandals, both gambling

and is known today only because of recent speculation that he was the notorious Jack the Ripper.

Yet Edward VII's popularity was immense. The British welcomed his lack of arrogance, his geniality and kindliness. Some seemed even to welcome his misbehavior after Queen Victoria's stern rectitude. Morever, overriding all misgivings, and immune to them, were certain assumptions by which Britain lived—that "progress" would continue and things would go on getting better because "science" would see to it that they did; that the white man was superior to all other men and that this was beyond question; that man—the white man, at any rate—was master of his fate, which meant that criminals deserved stark punishment and that the poor were poor because of their own shortcomings, although the "deserving poor" were suitable objects of charity; that social rank (the enshrinement of class) existed for good and sufficient reasons, and that if this was hard on social inferiors, there was no way out of that. These arrangements the Church of England sanctified. Its authority provided much of the cement that held the society together.

All of this (and more, for this was also the time of such writers as Wilde and Galsworthy, Arnold Bennett and Alfred Noyes) the term "Edwardian" signified. Edward himself was more important in his country's affairs than any monarch who followed him. He was instrumental in the conclusion of the Entente Cordiale between Britain and France, and by family contact tried to temper the ambitions of Kaiser Wilhelm and the German nation. This sort of activity by a British monarch is inconceivable today. So is most of Edwardian life, which survived the man for whom it was named by four years, until the outbreak of the First World War. Leslie Hamilton Wilson's photographs bring that life back to us almost as in a dream.

—Edwin Newman

and amorous, and when he became King, his liaison with a woman not his wife was far from a state secret. Nor was that all. His eldest son, Edward, Duke of Clarence, heir to the throne, was heir also to his father's playboy ways. He died at the age of 28,

Preface

Discovering the work of an unknown artist is always a satisfying feat. But when that work is an extraordinary portrait of an age rendered in vivid detail, artistic significance melds with historic importance. Such an unknown artist is Leslie Hamilton Wilson, a professional businessman of the Edwardian age who was an "amateur" photographer in the true sense of the word—as a lover of the art. Although "amateur" has acquired a contemporary connotation that is frivolous, in the late nineteenth and early twentieth centuries it was expected of a gentleman that he be skilled at some artistic pursuit. Significantly, many of the early photographers, as well as such turn of the century figures as Alexander Keighley, Frederick Evans and many others of the Photo-Secession and Linked Ring movements (schools of aesthetic photography) were likewise amateurs.

Wilson's prodigious work is something of a mystery. In scope, it represents a three-decade-long application to the photographic medium and a body of work that would rival the output of many "professional" photographers. But more surprising than their impressive volume is the quality of these images; they were excellent from the start, for Wilson's talent seems to have sprung full-blown from the time of his earliest endeavors.

Interestingly, in no other art form would a similar phenomenon be conceivable. Consider the likelihood of discovering an unknown composer of twenty masterly symphonies or a cache of ten novels by an accomplished unknown author. By contrast, photography until very recently was spared the weighty legitimacy of ART, making it possible to find an artist working with no consciousness of a public and no desire to relate to any tradition but his own. The creation of a photograph, like the writing of a diary, can be a personal experience which is rewarding on its own terms. If there is a certain self-indulgence to this endeavor, there is also a fundamental honesty which gives the work validity and historic significance. Our perceptions of the past are usually colored by someone else's point of view which may be ironic, satiric, nostalgic, romantic, expressionistic or even inaccurate. Seldom are we given the opportunity to see the past as itself, as objectively as is possible, given the Platonic limitations of first ascertaining reality and then being able to reproduce it accurately. In Wilson's photographs, we are introduced to the Edwardian world as it was perceived not by an historian, novelist or social critic, but by an Edwardian gentleman who had no motive other than pride and pleasure in his own experience.

It is difficult to position Wilson artistically. Was he an untutored primitive or a highly sophisticated artist? Certainly a man of his social class would have had a generous exposure to the fine arts, which would have included an awareness of the work of other photographers. Yet in his work he does not seem to have gone through the conventional stages of mimicking other artists before finding his own sense of style. This independence only deepens the enigma of why Wilson never sought to have his work recognized by others.

Though he lived and worked before and after the reign of

Edward VII, Leslie Hamilton Wilson's perceptions remained rooted in the spirit of that era. He was one of the few photographers to direct his camera at the foibles and passions of a society that unabashedly delighted in itself. And when that Age of Innocence finally dwindled to an end, Wilson focused his lens on the lingering traces of its afterglow. There are no definitive answers to the riddle of Wilson's accomplishment; although he left behind a photographic microcosm of the Edwardian era, we know little about the man himself, his motives or his aspirations. All that remain are the photographs and, fortunately for us, these require no explanation.

C.W.

An Edwardian Observer

But for one distinguishing passion, Leslie Hamilton Wilson was a perfect prototype of the upper-class Edwardian gentleman. A man of means, he lived graciously, traveled widely, and was a successful businessman who seemed content to blend anonymously into his social milieu. The unexpected dimension which brings this man to our attention is that he was also a photographer of extraordinary vision who, for more than thirty years (1895-1927), kept a photo-journal in which he documented his view of the world in which he lived. Indeed, Wilson's photographic legacy is one of the best records—and perhaps the only insider's view—of upper class life during the high point of British power before the First World War. Although his early exposure to the medium occurred mainly in the context of photographing family and friends engaged in the *divertissement* of Edwardian life, his interest soon became a serious artistic pursuit as Wilson discovered that his camera was an indispensable adjunct to his life. Accordingly, as he matured and refined his technique, his field of vision expanded to include landscape, travel photographs and increasingly reportorial or documentary images which anticipate by at least twenty years the photo-journalism of Erich Salomon or Cartier-Bresson. One can only marvel at the range of subjects which caught Wilson's eye: the Titanic before its launching, the great Belmonte in a Spanish bull-ring, Buffalo Bill on his last trip to the British Isles, the architecture of Gaudi in 1912, the doomed Scottish whaling industry, and a panoply of people and places that fascinated him in the course of his yearly travels.

The early twentieth century was a time of great innovation heralded by the introduction of the automobile and, later, the airplane. Wilson, intrigued by machinery (the camera itself is a machine), went up in one of the first planes to take flight over England and undertook countless motor excursions throughout northern Scotland. Since every trip necessitated some type of social visit, Wilson found himself in the position of perennial guest in a succession of Edwardian households, affording him ample opportunity to explore his craft. The elaborate social rituals which sprang up to accommodate the debut of the automobile were unending subjects of interest for the photographer. Picnics, sightseeing trips to the country, weekend parties, even fashions were stimulated and influenced by the new invention which also facilitated picture taking by providing an easy way to transport cumbersome equipment.

Leslie Hamilton Wilson had ready access to the activities and preoccupations of the upper class. Born in 1883, he was the son of an enterprising Scots merchant who had amassed his fortune in the commodities market. Young Wilson was raised in an atmosphere of privilege and comfort in which a man was judged not by his intrinsic worth but by his financial success. The tenor of the emergent nouveau riche society was described by the Countess of Cardigan as one "where money shouts and birth and breeding whisper." In imitation of the British artistocracy, this new class created a society predicated on charades of gentility. Favored pastimes were games involving the relentless pursuit of little balls, followed by the consumption of gargantuan meals, interspersed with periodic trips to France for the "season" and the endless social activity of life in town and country.

At the proper age, Wilson was duly dispatched to Harrow where he was introduced to photography. After completing his studies, he joined the family brokerage firm of Tod and Wilson, eventually succeeding sufficiently to become a founding partner in his own firm of Wilson, Scot and Co. in Glasgow. Like Wallace Stevens and Charles Ives, Wilson was first a businessman, then an artist. Perhaps it was necessary for him to fulfill the expectations demanded of him by his background and class before he could comfortably devote himself to his artistic pursuits. Since Wilson was primarily a social creature, his earliest photographic subjects were, predictably, his family and friends. In many ways, these images taken during "la belle epoque" are reminiscent of the work of Jacques Lartigue, who as a boy in France took to photography in much the same spirit as Wilson. But where Lartigue approached his work with an irreverent disrespect for permanence, Wilson strove to memorialize it. Where the young Frenchman delighted in capturing evanescent moments on film— candid shots of people caught off guard or in the midst of some activity—Wilson's concern was to chronicle and preserve a studied tableau of Edwardian society which would remain long after the era had ended. Nearly all of his photographs were captioned and handsomely bound in gilt-edged albums as if he intended from the outset to create an oeuvre which would immortalize his age.

If there is such a thing as a "talent for seeing," Wilson was certainly a prodigy imbued with an aesthetic eye. From the time of his earliest ventures into photography, he displayed an unerring instinct for simplifying, paring away the extraneous, and arriving at the essence of a subject in an uncannily direct way. This straightforward quality remained the essential characteristic of Wilson's work. Nevertheless, what seemed to be objectively apparent was filtered through a selective eye intensely influenced by the values of Edwardian society. Life, as seen in his photographs, was an extended garden party highlighted by race meets, hunts, fishing expeditions and golf and tennis tournaments. Wilson preferred to see everything from an ennobling perspective. Thus, in his images, meticulously uniformed soldiers are photographed at drill, laborers are viewed dutifully at work, gentlemen are invariably at sport and exquisitely groomed ladies are preferably in the bosom of their families. During the war, Wilson joined the 2/1 Ayrshire Yeomanry, serving for the duration as an officer and contributing his talents to the war effort by organizing a bicycle regiment! His photographs reveal none of the bloodshed or horror that culminated in his generation's premature demise in the trenches of France. One senses that Wilson chose not to see that which contradicted the rules of the game; instead he emphasized the camaraderie and fellowship of army life.

Whereas Wilson's social photography is closely observed, most often detailing some aspect of the diversions of the rich, his landscape work reveals the other side of his personality. Here we see the stark, brooding quality of the Scottish countryside where Wilson loved to walk and to escape from the hectic social activity which must frequently have become oppressive. Whereas earlier Victorian photographers preferred the sharp contrasts afforded by direct sunlight, Wilson skillfully utilized the muted light of overcast days to intensify the mood of Scotland's fog-shrouded mountains. Although his landscapes continue in the earlier traditions of such British topographical photographers as Valentine, Bedford and England, their interest to us lies in their subtle departures from the classic genre. Most of Wilson's photographs were printed on platinum paper, which may partially explain the repeated transformation of a picturesque scene into a curiously haunting image. The luminous quality and tonal delicacy of platinum are particularly well suited to the subject of the Scottish landscape and the play of light that Wilson favored. And of course, platinum is the most durable of photographic printing papers, which once again insured that these photographs would outlast their creator.

Like his predecessors, Wilson viewed a landscape in a formalistic way; each picture was divided into planes with carefully studied fore, middle and backgrounds and requisite proportions of sky, stone, vegetation or water. Despite these restrictive considerations, his landscapes present a view of nature which is more expansive than restrained.

Consider the photograph of *"An Dun"* (p. 59). In it, Wilson created a visual paradox in which at first glance all the elements have been reduced almost to abstraction, whereas on closer view, this quality serves to draw us into the picture and to make us part of the landscape itself. A stream bubbles in the middle of the photograph—it begins and ends nowhere; the boundaries of the mountains which frame the scene are likewise out of sight. First the eye is pulled downward to the mystery of the stream, then to a derelict boat marooned in the middle of nowhere, and finally onto a road leading off inscrutably into the distance. The composition is elegant yet the photograph has a disquieting effect. Landscape is portrayed as elemental, powerful and ultimately elusive.

This view is reinforced in *"On the Road to Seriska"* (p. 131). No setting is further removed from the Scottish countryside than the parched, attenuated landscape of Central India, but the photographer's eye has created a similar effect. Every component of this image has its origin beyond the confines of the picture, giving us the feeling that the photograph has begun somewhere else and will go on eternally. The hoofprints of vanished herds of cattle

intimate the ephemeral quality of life when juxtaposed with mountain and stream. In both photographs, the external simplicity and bareness belie a powerful undercurrent of feeling which appeals to our deepest perceptions of nature. Although neither image is as spectacular as an Ansel Adams landscape, it is a mark of Wilson's accomplishment that he is able to compel our attention in the starkest, most straightforward way.

From 1904 until 1927 (except for the years of World War I), Wilson devoted one to four months of each year to his travels, keeping detailed journals in which he drolly commented on the sights and circumstances he encountered. He withstood several harrowing escapades apparently bolstered by the stiff upper lip demanded of the proper Edwardian gentleman. In 1904, he was nearly trampled by an Egyptian racehorse; at Sarajevo, he foiled a would-be robber in his hotel room by producing a pistol from beneath his pillow; in Spain he narrowly missed being burned alive when the boiler in his hotel exploded—but all these incidents seemed to leave him with an increased appetite for adventure. The unflappable nature of the gentleman was partially due to his conviction that the strength of the British Empire would always protect him. A leading travel book of the time advised, "It should be observed that English is *always* understood if it is spoken clearly and accompanied by appropriate gestures of mime. His Majesty the King Emperor is personified in every Englishman abroad and orders must be given in a suitably imperious manner. Shout if necessary, but never dissemble. *God is your authority."* Armed with this resolve, Wilson was able to travel anywhere, see anything and remain emotionally unscathed. Throughout his travel photographs there is an air of the detached observer, the man who traveled compulsively as a means of escape but who seldom became involved with what he saw.

This attitude is subtly expressed in *"The Waterfront, Calcutta"*

(p. 127), a photograph which epitomizes the curious relationship of exotic places to the Western mentality. A procession of huge steel freighters looms ominously above a cluster of fragile native boats moored to the bank of the river; in that simple view lies a distilled vision of Europe and Asia in counterpoint. The contrast between the majestic force of the Empire and the insignificant vessels of its subject country is a visual symbol of the impact of colonialism. But there is another echo to this image, an implied sense of nostalgia as one realizes that the native boats are doomed to inertia while the European ships move on. In that inevitable movement, the Maugham-like ambiance of the Edwardian "at home in exile" would itself relinquish its place in an increasingly technological world.

Unfortunately for Wilson, the grand tour which was his dream was never made. He had planned to cross Russia by the Trans-Siberian Railway and then enter North China through the Great Wall, but unsettled political conditions after World War I made the trip impracticable. As a consolation, he accepted an invitation to visit Central India as a guest of the Maharajah of Alwar. Here, amidst fabulous wealth and opulence, Wilson and his party were transported to the countryside by a fleet of Rolls-Royces and entertained on a lavish scale by neighboring princes and maharajahs. This fittingly became Wilson's final trip and the epitome of the Edwardian style abroad. The quixotic flavor of the Anglo-Indian experience is perfectly captured in *"The Beaters"* (p. 146), a photograph which is instructive as well as technically interesting. The scene takes place after one of the Maharajah's state hunts in which his private army has acted as beater for the hunt. Standing at attention against a backdrop of eleven state elephants with their *mahouts,* the 250 soldiers look fiercely proud as if they had just been immortalized in great battle. It must have amused Wilson to realize that this photograph could never have been taken anywhere else. For where else but India could anyone command his army to take the morning off for a hunt? Where else could a mad maharajah* highlight the splendid excess of Mughal India with an army dressed in British khaki acting as his toy soldiers? This photograph is a timeless document of the power, prestige and fascination that princely India held for generations of Englishmen.

One of the most remarkable aspects of Wilson's photographs is that all of them were stimulated strictly by the artist's personal interests. It is difficult to think of another photographer who expended as much time and effort on what was, after all, a hobby, albeit a passionate one. Wilson devoted an entire volume of his photo-diary to the Scottish whaling industry. No one commissioned him to do this, nor were the photographs ever used for any documentary purpose, but they compare favorably with the most impressive work done by any of the professional photo-journalists. It was Wilson's intent to document the processes of the industry from the moment a whaling ship left the dock to the time (months later) that its final cargo was delivered to a harbor in England. He succeeded in doing this but managed also to transcend his subject at the same time.

A documentary photographer is often in the dubious position of being restricted by the very facts he is trying to convey. In order to propel the narrative, he must sometimes rely on a caption for clarification while the photograph is reduced to the secondary level of illustration. Wilson's whaling photographs are successful in that no words are required to elucidate the visual information. In addition to telling a story, these photographs are arresting images in which the harmony of all the elements is never sacri-

*Alwar was subsequently deposed because in addition to other improprieties, he preferred using live infants as bait on his hunts. "I never missed," he told a court of inquiry, "so what was the harm?"

ficed in order to make a point. Each photograph in this series can stand alone; each one rises above the specifics of the subject to become a composition similar to a landscape. Even in the photograph entitled *"Man on the Rendering Dock"* (p. 73), the workman making a ten-foot gash in the whale's abdomen does not detract from the elegant beauty of the whale itself or the sensual balance of the two figures in the frame.

It was characteristic of Wilson that he never lost his cool detachment from his subject. What replaces a sense of emotional involvement is a perfectly controlled sensibility in which classic restraint is used to full advantage. Today we have become accustomed to seeing photographs used as vehicles of propaganda, advertising or social protest. But Wilson as a photographer had no commitment to any cause save his desire to eloquently express his personal vision of the world around him. He chose to do this in an understated manner which was subtle, though direct. Throughout his life, Wilson remained a steadfast product of his age; his Edwardian perspective remained essentially unchanged despite repeated exposures to other cultures, new lifestyles and the basic changes wrought by time. He died in 1968 (at the age of 85) at his home in Ayr, Scotland. Wilson outlived the era he had documented by almost half a century so that his journals must have become ghostly echoes of his past. Enigmatically, Wilson gave up photography after his last trip to India. This coincided with the year when it became virtually impossible to obtain fresh supplies of platinum printing paper, and perhaps that objectively defined for Wilson the end of that era which had given his work a thematic frame of reference. In all of his images, Wilson strove to illuminate the quintessence of his subject—that aspect which was most simple and permanent. When it was no longer feasible to present his material in the manner he deemed appropriate, Wilson chose not to compromise and retired from the field.

There is no evidence that during his lifetime, Leslie Hamilton Wilson ever attempted to exhibit his photographs, nor is there any indication that he ever showed them to anyone. For Wilson, the camera became a way of communicating with himself as he catalogued, perfected and secreted away all the moments he had lived. He was a remarkable collector whose treasury was composed not of stamps or shells, but of the experiences of his life. In a sense, his entire work was his diary, but instead of being lifeless snapshots of purely personal interest, Wilson's photographs are a vivid document of a time of grace and style that will never be recaptured. As such, they acquire a haunting life of their own while enriching our understanding and appreciation of the Edwardian moment.

—Clark Worswick

The Edwardian Scene

We return with Svend Bruun   *Friday, 27th February*

Railway termini . . . are our gates to the glorious and the unknown. Through them we pass out into adventure and sunshine, to them, alas! we return. In Paddington all Cornwall is latent and the remoter west; down the inclines of Liverpool Street lie fenlands and the illimitable Broads; Scotland is through the pylons of Euston; Wessex behind the poised chaos of Waterloo.

—E. M. Forster

Enid

The king and queen

This wonderful year! We already have Coronation Exhibitions, Coronation Bibles, Coronation Dances, and for all we know, Coronation Dog Fights, and now, in addition to these, it seems there is to be a Coronation Ceremony at Westminster Abbey. The Coronation Ceremony, by-the-way, promises to be the most successful function of the year. In addition to a host of notabilities, the King and Queen have promised to be present.

—*Punch*

Kippendavie

You must take three times as many frocks as the number of days for which you stay. Thus if you are there a week, you will want twenty-one in all, since the men do not like the women to wear the same thing again. You will want seven shooting costumes, or, if you don't shoot, seven tailor-mades for shooting lunches, seven tea-gowns and seven evening-gowns. Throw in a few more in case of anything special.

—*Punch*

H. J. W. and W. W.   Golden Wedding

Darling, I am growing old,
Silver threads among the gold
Shine upon my brow to-day;
Life is fading fast away.
                    —Eben Rexford

George Boyd, Kerr and Percy Symington

A young Scotsman of your ability let loose upon the world with £300, what could he not do? It's almost appalling to think of; especially if he went among the English.

—James Barrie

L. M. Moriarty

No bubble is so iridescent or floats longer than that blown by the successful teacher.

—William Ernest Henley

Forty years on, when afar and asunder
Parted are those who are singing to-day.
          —Edward Ernest Bowen

Old fourth form room, Harrow

Alloway   *Burns Monument*

There once was a man who said 'Damn!
It is borne in upon me I am
An engine that moves
In predestinate grooves
I'm not even a bus I'm a tram.'
—Maurice Hare

Peace celebrations   *Boer War*

My ghost

Lunch at the Roman Camp

Whether these repasts are served in the open field or in a country house, the man in charge of the hampers must be extremely careful not to forget any of the accessories of the meal. It often happens that on going to open the champagne it is found that the packer forgot to include a corkscrew and wire-nippers, or perhaps the glasses, the bread, the salt or the salad dressing. These contretemps tend to mar the best appointed of repasts. To prevent this, a list should be made the previous day of all the provisions and everything necessary to make a really nice service, and then ticked off as they are placed in the hamper.

—J. Rey

Miss Boyd is rather particular about her lunch

MENU FOR AN "AL-FRESCO" LUNCHEON

Hors-d-Oeuvre Variés

Mayonnaise de Saumon
Médaillons de Homard à la Russe

Boeuf braisé à la Gelée
Jambon d'York
Poulet Rôti   Langue a l'Ecarlate
Galantine de Volaille
Pâté de Foie Gras Truffé
Suprèmes de Volaille St. James
Salade Coeurs de Laitues

Gelée Macédoine
Crème Parisienne
Gâteau Princesse
Blancmange aux Amandes
Pâtisserie assortis

Dessert

Café

A pic-pic car with Uncle James and Nurse

Colonel Cody (Buffalo Bill)

Willie speaking to Captain and Mrs. Crowshaw

I suppose society is wonderfully delightful. To be in it is merely a bore.
But to be out of it simply a tragedy.

—Oscar Wilde

There is only one thing in the world worse than being talked about, and that is not being talked about.

—Oscar Wilde

Tea at the races

John A. Holms on "Actress"

Lord Eglinton's foxhounds

The English country gentleman galloping after a fox—the unspeakable in full pursuit of the uneatable.

—Oscar Wilde

Some of the party

Mankind is divisible into two great classes: hosts and guests.
—Sir Max Beerbohm

Miss Stouart and Miss Glover

GOLF VICTOR!

The girls crave for freedom, they cannot endure
  To be cramped up at Tennis in courts that are poky.
And they're all of them certainly, perfectly sure
  That they'll never again touch 'that horrible Croquet',
Where it's quite on the cards that they play with Papa,
And where all that goes on is surveyed by Mamma.

To Golf on the downs for the whole of the day
  Is 'awfully jolly', they keep on asserting,
With a good-looking fellow to teach you the way,
  And to fill up the time with some innocent flirting;
And it may be the maiden is wooed and is won,
E'er the whole of the round is completed and done.
                                        —Punch

St. Andrews   *Abe Mitchell*

Golf gives more oportunities to the dressy man than any other pastime. Football and cricket reduce every one to a dead level in dress, but in golf there is any amount of scope for individuality in costume. The burning question which divides golfers into two hostile camps is the choice between knickerbockers and trousers . . . to a man with a really well-turned calf and neat ankles I should say, wear knickerbockers whenever you get a chance. Knickerbockers afford great scope for the display of stylish stockings. A very good effect is produced by having a little red tuft which should appear under the roll which surmounts the calf. The roll itself, which should always have a smart pattern, is very useful in conveying the impression that the calf is more fully developed than it really is.

—Punch

Elsie Boyd drives the first green

Battleby   The house party

Muriel Wylie Hill

Miss McCulloch receiving the championship cup

"Father, Mother and Me,
Sister and Auntie say,
All the people like us are We
And everyone else is They."
　　　　　—Rudyard Kipling

The headmaster and Miss Wood

Loch Ness near Fort Augustus

Mr. Boyds Renault

FAIRPLAY FOR MOTORISTS

Dear Sir,—Why should motorists alone be obliged to give warning of their approach at cross roads and corners? The only efficient way to minimize collisions is to insist that all who use the roads should make their advent audible. Horsemen should have a bell or horn affixed to the pummel of their saddles, while pedestrians should have a similar means of signalling attached to the handles of their sticks and umbrellas. The loneliness of the open road, which so often affects the spirits of dwellers in the country, would thus be sensibly mitigated, and the burden of precaution equitably distributed between the tortoises and the hares of modern life.

Yours faithfully,   F.I.A.T. Justitia   The Reeks, Leighton Buzzard

—Punch

INCONSIDERATE ANIMALS.

Dear Sir,—The stupidity of animals is one of the greatest curses of a residence in the country, as I have long found out to my cost. When motoring at the rate of thirty miles an hour or upwards one can generally count on pedestrians keeping out of the middle of the road. But it is otherwise with poultry, sheep, and even young rabbits. Only yesterday I had a new Michelin tyre seriously damaged by a hedgehog and last week my wife was struck in the face by a clumsy sparrow which, if she had not been wearing goggles, might have done her serious mischief. As it was she was so much upset that she was unable to play Bridge for several hours.

Faithfully yours, Max Bamberger.   Bungalow deLuxe,   Little Slanton

—Punch

Ballachulish *The ferry*

Kerr B. Symington

Brooklands   *L. H. W. takes a flight with Raynham*

Hendon   Louis Noel at the wheel of a biplane   (70 hp)

Last week M. Bleriot flew the Channel in half an hour—thirty-three minutes to be exact. Mr. H. Latham has tried it twice and failed. The first time he fell into the sea and was rescued by following vessels. I agree with Shackleton that these things represent a foolish waste of money. Besides, flying across the Channel means nothing after you have done it. You can't carry goods or passengers.

—R.D.B.'s "Diary" Aug. 25, 1909

DAMOCLES UP-TO-DATE

When overhead the airships fly
  In countless swarms by day and night
And locust-like obscure the sky
  And dim the heavenly bodies' light,
What will the joy of life be worth
To us who still must tread the earth?

How shall we dare to stay at home
  In villa, mansion, flat or cot,
When shipwrecked aeronauts may come
  Unbidden down the chimney pot;
And slight mishaps to ropes and gears
Hustle the house about our ears?

Abroad a rain of oil and slops
  Will wreck the smartest hats and gowns,
While anchor flukes uproot the crops
  Or sweep the golfer off his downs,
And grapnels hook up to the skies
The angler hoping for a rise.

When feasters in the ether fling
  From dizzy heights a crust of bread
Or fragments of a chicken's wing,
  To drop, by gravity, like lead,
The deadly hail will penetrate
Umbrellas made of armour-plate.

                    —Punch

Hendon   *L. H. W. takes his first flight*

Titanic

L. H. W. photographing the falls

THE WILD SWANS AT COOLE

The trees are in their autumn beauty,
The woodland paths are dry,
Under the October twilight the water
Mirrors a still sky;
Upon the brimming water among the stones
Are nine-and-fifty swans.

The nineteenth autumn has come upon me
Since I first made my count;
I saw, before I had well finished,
All suddenly mount
And scatter wheeling in great broken rings
Upon their clamorous wings.

I have looked upon those brilliant creatures,
And now my heart is sore.
All's changed since I, hearing at twilight,
The first time on this shore,
The bell-beat of their wings above my head,
Trod with a lighter tread.

Unwearied still, lover by lover,
They paddle in the cold
Companionable streams or climb the air;
Their hearts have not grown old;
Passion or conquest, wander where they will,
Attend upon them still.

But now they drift on the still water
Mysterious, beautiful;
Among what rushes will they build,
By what lake's edge or pool
Delight men's eyes when I awake some day
To find they have flown away?

—William Butler Yeats

56

Swans on Castlehill Pond

An Dun

The Nith near Thornhill

Dalmally   Angus and E. M. Collins

"The Ritz Hotel"

Donald has a spy

ROADWAYS

One road leads to London,
One road runs to Wales,
My road leads me seawards
To the white dripping sails.

One road leads to the river,
As it goes singing slow;
My road leads to shipping,
Where the bronzed sailors go.

Leads me, lures me, calls me
To salt green tossing sea;
A road without earth's road-dust
Is the right road for me.

—John Masefield

Whaling

It were better to admit at once that there are two kinds of whales: the whales that are classified as cetaceans, and those that are enlarged into ideas. The former are biological specimens or commercial propositions; the latter belong to a race longer-lived, changed in colour as the white whale, Moby Dick, or changed in form as the dragon, the undying serpent, but, however changed, representing the something in the sea of which we feel afraid.

—P. V. Morley & J. S. Hodgson

Whales seem to be such good beasts, and have such kind brown eyes—nothing of the fish in them, and their colouring is that of all the sea; their backs are grey-black to dove-colour, reflecting the blue of the sky, and the white of their underside is like the white of a kid glove with the faintest pink beneath, so white it makes the sea-foam look grey as it washes across it to and fro, and the white changes to emerald-green in the depths to the blue-green of an iceberg's foot. It is strange that this skin should be so extremely delicate in such a large animal; it is too thin to be used as leather.

—W. G. Burn Murdoch

A couple of small sperm whales

When the stage is ready, the whales are hauled inshore and up, the heavy winches straining and the tackle singing under the load. When the carcass is in position, the flensing begins. With flensing-knives the size and shape of hockey-sticks, but razor-edged, parallel cuts are made in the hard blubber, from head to tail; and the strips of white blubber—between a foot or eighteen inches wide and (for the fin-whale) four to six inches thick—are pulled off by the winch. It is not easy to cut the blubber; it is of the consistency of a hard rubber ball; it is firm, and your foot rebounds if you kick it.

—P. V. Morley & J. S. Hodgson

Look on that vast outline once more. Never in the old days could men see the whale, as we can see him now, and say, thus was he made. . . . Where went that spirit, which played in this magnificence—which made this mountain leap and sport, quickened the eye, retracted that balloon of tongue, lifted that fallen jaw? This was a lump which solved some wild equation of the elements. This monstrous form and painted shapeliness has burned its way through phosphorescent waves in summer, the black night lighted by luminous clouds of its own breathing; and sinking with an easy silence, it has spiralled to unseen depths, upon unknown desires.

—P. V. Morley & J. S. Hodgson

Man on the Rendering Dock

The whole of the whale's body is used. The best of the meat is sent to Copenhagen, bought by Danish butchers at the stations for 18s. a barrel, sold at Copenhagen as a delicacy at £9 a barrel. It is very good to eat—between beef and veal, but rather better than either. The Japanese pay 25 cents a pound for it, but we use it for fertilizing fields. The oil extracted from the blubber, meat and bone, sells now at about £4 a barrel; six barrels equal, roughly, a ton (2240 lb). But the value of whale oil is increasing owing to the invention of a "hardening" process by which the oil is turned into white tasteless edible fat excellent for cooking purposes.

—W. G. Burn Murdoch

Glasgow   The S.S. Esperanca arrives with 13,700 barrels of oil
from West Africa, the product of 760 whales

World War I

The gas helmet race

Owing to the Glasgow Stock Exchange being closed during the first three months of the war, business was conducted in the street.

L. H. W.s tent

You are ordered abroad as a soldier of the King to help our French comrades against the invasion of a common enemy. You have to perform a task which will need your courage, your energy, your patience. Remember that the honour of the British Army depends on your individual conduct. It will be your duty not only to set an example of discipline and perfect steadiness under fire but also to maintain the most friendly relations with those whom you are helping in this struggle. In this new experience you may find temptations both in wine and women. You must entirely resist both temptations and, while treating all women with perfect courtesy, you should avoid any intimacy. Do your duty bravely. Fear God. Honour the King.

—Horatio Herbert, Earl Kitchener

The 9th Cyclist Brigade inspected by Field Marshall Lord French

A Sopwith "Pup" in difficulties

Officers bayonet class

The "C" 15

The Lewis gun section

To set the cause above renown,
To love the game beyond the prize,
To honor, while you strike him down,
The foe that comes with fearless eyes;
To count the life of battle good
And dear the land that gave you birth,
And dearer yet the brotherhood
That binds the brave of all the earth.

—Sir Henry Newbolt

The signalling officer   J.F.P. MacLaren

"Spy hunting" near Tyringham Village

Pizzy teaches us how to make a jam tin bomb

The 1st Line entraining en route for Gallipoli

What is our task? To make Britain a fit country for heroes to live in.

The stern hand of fate has scourged us to an elevation where we can see the great everlasting things that matter for a nation; the great peaks of honour we had forgotten—duty and patriotism clad in glittering white; the great pinnacle of sacrifice pointing like a rugged finger to Heaven.

—David Lloyd George

S. S. 143 The artillery barrage

Travel

The sphinx and pyramid of Kephren

Port Said

While in Cairo this morning I took particular notice of the various costumes worn by the Arabs. The old custom still prevails to a certain extent of distinguishing the different sects and grades of society, by the colour and shape of their turbans. The Sherifs, or descendants of the prophet wear white turbans; while green ones are worn by pilgrims who have been to Mecca. Copts (Christians) usually wear a white turban put on in coils and a black costume. The proper length of a turban should be seven times the length of the wearers' head, in order to act as his winding-sheet when dead. The ordinary native goes about bare footed, wears white pants, and over them a long blue shirt like a night-gown; on his head a small round white cap. The poor women wear pretty much the same costume, but in their case dispense with the pants; on their bare feet and arms they usually wear a few silver and copper bracelets, and a black mask that covers the face up to the eyes. . . . Among the lower classes, it is a common practice with both men and women to tattoo the chin, arms and chest.

—L. H. Wilson

East and West

Making bricks

W. W.'s picnic at the lower barrage

The day of small nations has long passed away. The day of Empires has come.

—Joseph Chamberlain

We took our new dragoman Saleh Achmet to show us the Mouski. Of all the sights I have seen the hardest to describe is the Mouski. It is really more than a street, it is a quarter wherein wind and interwind dozens of small alleys, crowded with every description of native life. The Mouski proper is a long straight throughfare that traverses the whole length of the old town, and is bisected half way by the Khalig Street. It is crowded to excess with natives, who form one ceaseless flow of many coloured and voiced humanity. Carriages can only proceed at a walk, and even then the driver has continually to call out warnings. One can hardly move a yard without hearing some of the following expressions: "riglak, riglak efendi" (take care, take care sir), "û â shemâlak" (look out, on the left), "yemînak ya sheikh" (to your right, Oh chief). Every now and then a mule lumbers past, adding greatly to the confusion.

—L. H. Wilson

Miss Cauthon Miss Carey Mrs. Carey W. W.

Tangier   *Changing guard at the harbour gate*

An acrobatic performance

Date palms near Marakesh

Our passports are examined at the frontier

Rua del Villar

View from Montserrat

On account of its cotton and silk mills, machine factories, dye works and iron foundries, it (Barcelona) is a very wealthy city. This can be seen from its handsome balconied houses and wide boulevards. Some of the architecture is extraordinary. One church which is in course of being built has every kind of fish, insect, reptile, bird and beast carved on the walls as well as angels and devils; while some of the private houses are designed to represent cave dwellings etc. Others again are plastered over with coloured tiles of peculiar design.

—L. H. Wilson

Barcelona   Curious architecture

Cadiz   Grand Hotel de Paris et de France

Interior of the bull ring

Another feat of strength

Belmonte takes a risk

Bull fighters like their victims are nearly all Andalusians. They are easily recognized in the street by the pigtails they wear. A curious thing about a Matador is that he has no special training. It is erroneous to think that at one time he must have been a Toreador then a Picador and Bandillero. Most of them are recruited from the Bandilleros, but as a rule, once a Toreador always a Toreador. The same applies to Picadors. At present the public have gone mad over a new Matador called Belmonte, who so far has not appeared in a first class ring. Two years ago he was a stonebreaker, but some Spanish George Edwards "discovered" him and put him into one of his rings last year, and the result is that he is now one of the people's idols.

—L. H. Wilson

A corner of the Lion Court

Barcelona   The Ramblas

Canal Grande

St. Mark's Cathedral

Venice

Dalmatia

One old couple who sat opposite to us at lunch were most amusing to watch. The soup course passed off all right, but when the entree was served (it was really a course of hors d'oeuvres) the old gentleman put his nose into each, grunted like a pig and then cleared nearly everything into his plate, but left one sardine for his wife, who for several moments handled the various knives and forks, evidently not quite sure which to use. Her husband's advice having been asked she started on the sardine, but presently changed her mind about the fork she was using and took up another, which when the old fellow noted, he bent over and took it out of her hand, and substituted the original.

The meat course next caused some difficulty, but having grasped their knives in one hand (after changing from one hand to the other several times) and knitting the fingers of their other hands round the forks they started off; the old lady preferring to use her knife to convey the food to her mouth, while the husband gobbled his down so fast that his hands appeared to be working like a pair of chop sticks.

Chicken was next served and along with it a small glass bowl for stewed fruit: the old lady first having almost deposited the fruit on her plate, suddenly guessed what the bowl was for just in time. Judging from the way she looked up and the smile she gave us, one could almost hear her say, "My word what a near shave." . . . An ice then followed with which the husband managed to cover his fingers; these he first sucked, then wiped them on the table cloth. . . . Meanwhile his wife, not risking the ice, was trying to blow her nose on her napkin . . . noticing she had not taken the stewed fruit with the chicken, she conveyed the bowl to her mouth, and started eating with one side of her mouth, while she put out the stones at the other. We left when coffee had been served and the last thing I saw were two spoons standing triumphantly up in the coffee cups, while the old folks were smacking their lips with satisfaction.

—L. H. Wilson

Our fellow passengers on the Bosnia

CARGOES

Quinquireme of Nineveh from distant Ophir
Rowing home to haven in sunny Palestine,
With a cargo of ivory,
And apes and peacocks,
Sandalwood, cedarwood, and sweet white wine.

Stately Spanish galleon coming from the Isthmus,
Dipping through the Tropics by the palm-green shores,
With a cargo of diamonds,
Emeralds, amethysts,
Topazes, and cinnamon, and gold moidores.

Dirty British coaster with a salt-caked smoke stack,
Butting through the Channel in the mad March days,
With a cargo of Tyne coal,
Road-rails, pig-lead,
Firewood, iron-ware, and cheap tin trays.

—John Masefield

The Waterfront, Calcutta

Our special train at Sheikh Othman

A caravan from Kabul

During the first two or three days of his service it should be carefully explained to the travelling servant exactly what he is expected to do. . . . A travelling servant who can speak English is almost indispensable for those who travel by road or train, but should not be engaged except on the recommendation of a trustworthy Agent, such as Cox and King's, Thos. Cook & Son . . . he may be exchanged at Delhi or Calcutta if ill or unsatisfactory. Such a servant is necessary to wait on his master in hotel bedrooms, and will be very useful in a hundred different ways.

—*A Handbook for Travellers in India*

On the road to Seriska

The tank behind the city palace

The Taj from the Great Gateway

A cotton ginner

Gwalior

My luggage arrives at Khera Camp

Travellers who leave the beaten track with the intention of shooting . . . should take a small tent or two with them. Transport, in the shape of camels, carts, baggage-ponies, or bearers, can be got in any station, and in the larger places riding ponies and light native carts or perhaps even European traps for driving can be obtained . . . perhaps the following suggestions of requirements may prove of some use in the case of a solitary traveller who does not mind a certain amount of roughing. . . . Tent . . . for self, and if cold or likely to be wet, a *pal* tent for servants—a few iron tent pegs . . . and a mallet. Camp-bed with side poles of one piece, table, chairs and carpet. India-rubber flat bath, and a board to stand on, or one's tubbing can be done by pouring native pots of water over head . . . a screen . . . to use as a bath-room. . . .

—*A Handbook for Travellers in India*

Closing in on the pig

A man may have slain his hundreds of tigers, he may have killed a hecatomb of big game in Africa and elsewhere, but if he has not followed the mighty boar, he has not tested the delights of the most fascinating and invigorating sport in the world. Anyone may kill a tiger by potting him from a tree or a *machan,* but it requires a *man* to ride down, and spear, a boar.

The vicissitudes and dangers of the sport are many. Man and horse are pitted against one of the most plucky and savage of wild beasts. The ground is generally execrable; there can be no craning; a hunter of the boar must ride not only straight, but his hardest, if he intends to try conclusions with his foe.

—Colonel Pollock

Khera Camp

My morning bath arrives

Our jungle wine cellar

The coolest spot in camp

Ready to start for a tiger drive

The beaters

L. H. W. about to shoot a sambur

The panther, a female 6 foot 6 inches

A man travels the world over in search of what he needs and returns home to find it.

—George Moore

Credits

Page

17   E. M. Forster, *Howard's End,* London, Edward Arnold, 1910.

19   *Punch,* June 7, 1911, London, Bradbury, Agnew & Co., Ltd.

21   *Punch,* March 2, 1904, London, Bradbury, Agnew & Co., Ltd.

22   Eben Rexford, "Silver Threads Among the Gold," *Pansies and Rosemary,* Philadelphia, J. B. Lippincott Co., 1910.

23   Sir James M. Barrie, *What Every Woman Knows, A Comedy,* London, Nodder & Stoughton, 1918.

24   W. E. Henley, *The Works of W. E. Henley,* London, D. Nutt, 1908.

25   Edward Ernest Bowen, "Forty Years On, Harrow Football Song," *Harrow Songs and Other Verses,* London, Longmans & Co., 1886.

26   Maurice Hare, Oxford, 1905.

29   J. Rey, *The Whole Art of Dining,* London, Carmona & Baker, 1914.

30   Ibid.

33   Oscar Wilde, *A Woman of No Importance,* London, John Lane, 1894.

34   Oscar Wilde, *The Picture of Dorian Gray,* London, Ward Lock & Co., 1891.

37   Oscar Wilde, *A Woman of No Importance,* London, John Lane, 1894.

38   Sir Max Beerbohm, "Hosts and Guests," *And Even Now,* London, W. Heinemann, 1921.

39   *Punch,* March 2, 1904, London, Bradbury, Agnew & Co., Ltd.

40   Ibid.

44   Rudyard Kipling, "We and They," *The Oxford Dictionary of Quotations,* London, Oxford University Press, 1941.

47   *Punch,* May 2, 1906, London, Bradbury, Agnew & Co., Ltd.

48   Ibid.

52   R. D. B.'s "Diary," August 25, 1909, Quoted in James Laver, *An Edwardian Promenade,* London, Edward Hulton & Co., Ltd., 1958.

53   *Punch,* May 29, 1907, London, Bradbury, Agnew & Co., Ltd.

56   William Butler Yeats, *The Wild Swans at Coole,* London, Macmillan and Co., 1919.

65   John Masefield, "Roadways," *The Story of a Round-House,* New York, Macmillan and Co., 1912.

67   P. V. Morley and J. S. Hodgson, *Whaling North and South,* London, Methuen & Co., Ltd., 1927.

68   W. G. Burn Murdoch, *Modern Whaling and Bear-Hunting,* London, Seeley, Service & Co., 1917.

71   Ibid.

72   P. V. Morley and J. S. Hodgson, *Whaling North and South,* London, Methuen & Co., Ltd., 1927.

75   W. G. Burn Murdoch, *Modern Whaling and Bear-Hunting,* London, Seeley, Service & Co., 1917.

84   Horatio Herbert Kitchener, Earl Kitchener, "A Message to be Kept by Each British Soldier in His Active Service Pay-Book," 1914.

80   Sir Henry Newbolt, *The Island Race,* New York, John Lane, 1899.

94   David Lloyd George, Earl of Dwyfor, "Honour and Dishonour," Speech delivered at the Queen's Hall, London, September 19, 1914.

98   Leslie Hamilton Wilson, *Travel Journal,* 1904.

101 Joseph Chamberlain, Speech, Birmingham, May 12, 1904.

102 Leslie Hamilton Wilson, *Travel Journal,* 1904.

113 Ibid., 1913.

117 Ibid.

124 Ibid., 1912.

126 John Masefield, "Cargoes," *The Story of a Round-House,* New York, Macmillan and Co., 1912.

130 *A Handbook for Travellers in India,* London, John Murray, 1905.

140 Colonel Pollock, *Fifty Years Reminiscence in India,* London, 1899.

141 *A Handbook for Travellers in India,* London, John Murray, 1905.

149 George Moore, *The Brook Kerith, A Syrian Story,* Edinburgh, T. Werner Laurie, 1916.

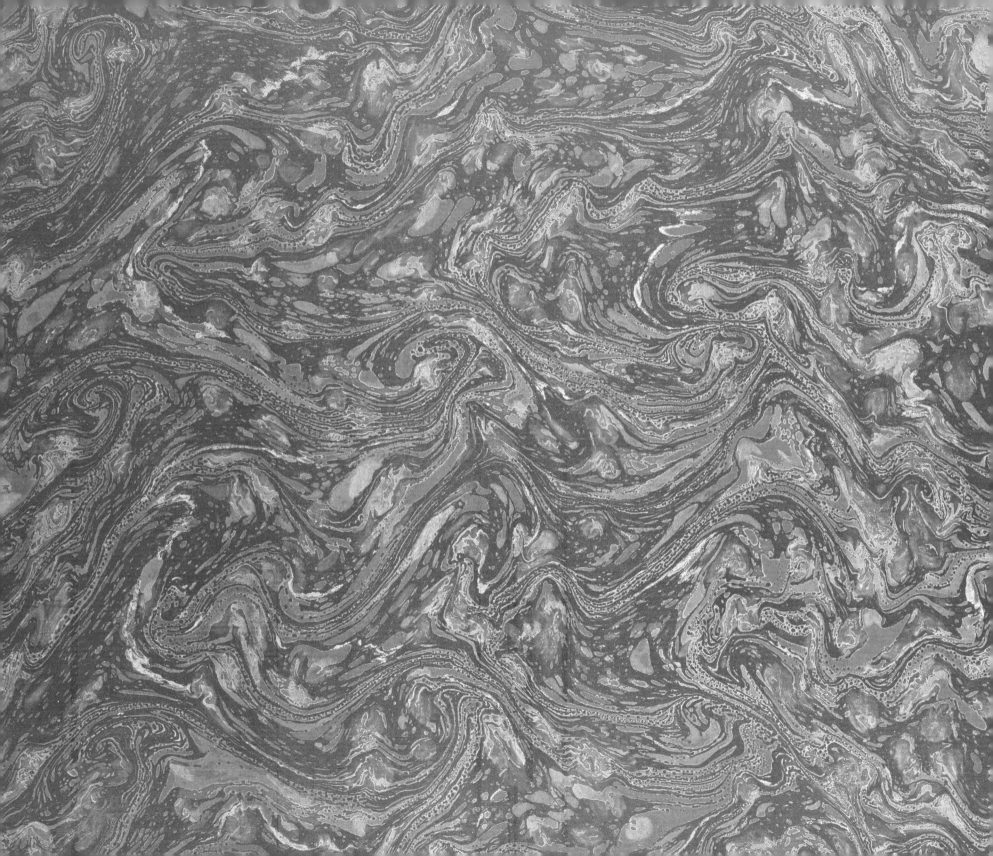